"I AM"
AFFIRMATIONS
FOR KIDS

Written by Jerrica Alexander
Illustrated by Mary Marsh

ISBN: 978-0-578-90674-4

I AM KIND...

I treat others the way I want to be treated, no matter what. Sometimes it's tough and other times it's easy, but no matter what I do my best!

I can handle anything that comes my way. I may get frustrated or tired but I push through. I am powerful beyond measure.

I AM HONEST...

I do the right thing even when no one is watching. I speak the truth even when it is hard. My parents remind me everyday to do the right thing and I remind myself when I am tempted to make bad choices.

I AM FOCUSED...

I concentrate on the things I want
to accomplish even when it gets tough.
It is okay to feel overwhelmed but
I always focus on what is true:
I can handle anything!

I AM SMART...

I listen and observe the things around me to take as much knowledge as possible and apply what I have learned. I am becoming brighter and brighter everyday!

I AM CREATIVE...

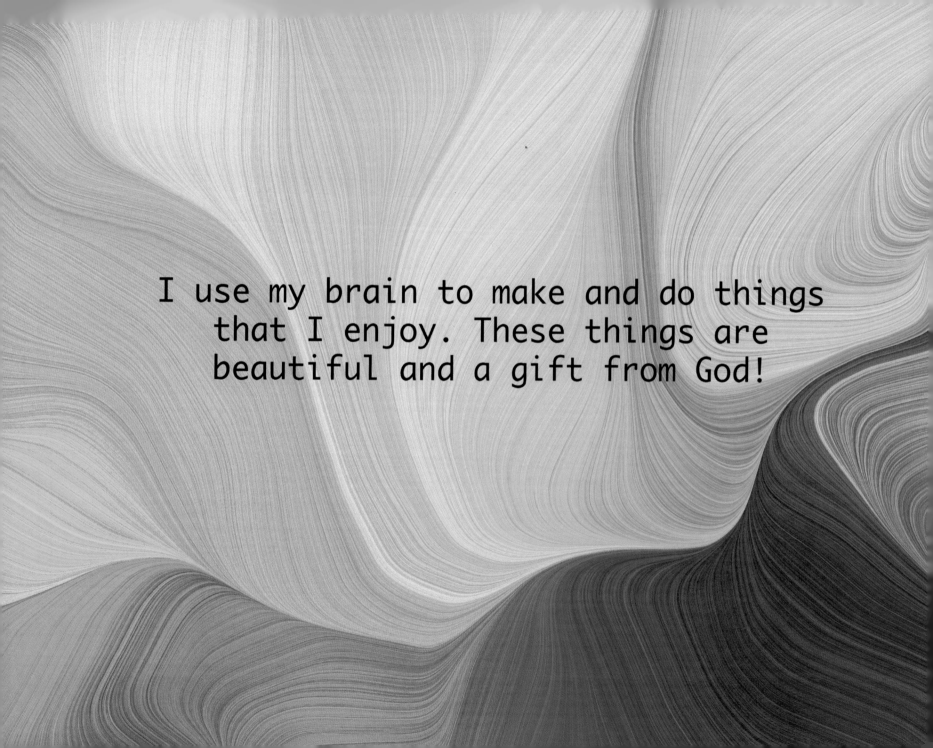

I use my brain to make and do things that I enjoy. These things are beautiful and a gift from God!

I AM PROUD...

I feel happy when I accomplish things.
I please myself as well as my parents.
When I complete my tasks I reward
myself with a treat!

I AM LOVE...

I use my smile and kindness to spread joy to others. I radiate a positive attitude even on not so good days!

I AM GRATEFUL...

I am thankful for the people around me like my family and friends. I also have a warm bed and toys to play with. This is awesome!

I face my fears or things that may
make me feel uncomfortable or
scared. I build up the courage
and get it done because
I CAN DO ANYTHING!

I AM Jerrica Alexander.

I am from Cahokia, Illinois by way of East Saint Louis, Illinois. I am married and have two children, a boy and a girl. I am a graduate of Southern Illinois university of Edwardsville where I gained a love for children while studying education in my undergraduate studies. I have taught for a decade in urban education in the metropolitan area of Saint Louis, Missouri.

My inspiration for children's books comes from two places: my love for writing and my love for children. Writing has always been an outlet for me and I finally decided to share. I love this book because it was born during a difficult time of remote learning for my daughter. We got through our tough times together by sharing positive affirmations. My hope is that this helps other families and children. My goal is to create a positive train of thought in every child that this book reaches. I want you to know that you can do anything you work hard at!